Lord, May Our Hearts Be Fertile Ground

Singing a Response to the Parables

MILBURN PRICE

MACON, GEORGIA

Lord, May Our Hearts Be Fertile Ground
Singing a Response to the Parables

Published by Celebrating Grace, Inc.
Copyright © 2017 by Celebrating Grace, Inc.
6501 Peake Road
Building 800
Macon, Georgia 31210
(877) 550-7707

ISBN 978-1-936151-18-9 (paperback edition)
ISBN 978-1-936151-19-6 (EPUB Edition)

All rights reserved. No part of this work may be reproduced transmitted or distributed in any form or by any means, electronic or mechanical, including photocopying and recording, or stored in a data base or retrieval system, without the prior written permission of the publisher, except in the case of brief quotations embodied in critical reviews and certain other noncommercial uses permitted by copyright law. Requests for permission should be addressed to Celebrating Grace, Inc., Permissions Office, 6501 Peake Road, Building 800, Macon, Georgia 31210.

For information about special discounts available for bulk purchases, sales promotions, fund-raising and educational needs, contact Celebrating Grace at (877) 550-7707 or inquiries@celebrating-grace.com.

Cover design and interior layout by Julie Hodgins

Scripture quotations are from the following sources:

The Holy Bible, Berean Study Bible, BSB, Copyright © 2016 by Bible Hub. Used by permission. All Rights Reserved Worldwide.

THE HOLY BIBLE, NEW INTERNATIONAL VERSION®. Copyright © 1973, 1978, 1984, 2011 by Biblica, Inc. Used by permission. All rights reserved worldwide.

Scripture quotations taken from the *NEW AMERICAN STANDARD BIBLE®* (NASB), Copyright © 1960, 1962, 1963, 1968, 1971, 1972, 1973, 1975, 1977, 1995 by the Lockman Foundation. Used by permission. www.Lockman.org

Scripture quotations are from *New Revised Standard Version Bible,* copyright © 1989 National Council of the Churches of Christ in the United States of America. Used by permission. All rights reserved worldwide.

17 18 19 20 21 22 23 24 – 10 9 8 7 6 5 4 3 2 1
Manufactured in the United States of America

Contents

Introduction	4
Lord, May Our Hearts Be Fertile Ground	7
Who Is My Neighbor?	9
O Lord, Your Word Has Come to Us	11
Praying Christ, We Hear Your Word	13
From Tiny Seed of Mustard	15
Jesus, Shepherd of the Flock	17
You Should Build on Firm Foundations	19
Take What I Give and Use It Well	21
How Much Is Enough?	23
Who Was the Prodigal?	25
Lord, May Our Hearts Be Fertile Ground - *Hymn*	26
Who Was the Prodigal? - *Hymn*	27

Introduction

Theologians and biblical scholars have often referred to a pattern of "revelation and response" that constitutes an essential aspect of Christian worship. Within that pattern, those who gather for worship encounter revelation through scripture, symbols, prayer, preaching, and other means. Worshipers, in turn, respond to revelation in a variety of ways. One of the most prevalent, and obvious, vehicles for response is congregational song.

In his teaching and preaching, Jesus often used parables as "means of revelation." The purpose of this small collection is to provide a few hymns that, hopefully, will be useful for congregations to sing as their response to the reading of and/or preaching on selected parables. In some instances, phrases from the parable appear in the parallel hymn text. In others, the hymn text comments on the teaching of the parable without quoting from it. In still other instances, allusions appear to other related biblical passages.

This project began when I was asked to write a hymn (text and tune) celebrating the fifteenth anniversary of Dr. Gary Furr's pastorate at Vestavia Hills Baptist Church in Vestavia Hills, Alabama. In addition to Dr. Furr's insightful and effective preaching, his wife, Vickie, makes a significant contribution to that family of faith through her teaching of an adult Sunday School class. For that occasion I found myself drawn to the parable of the sower and the seed as the foundation for a hymn ("Lord, May Our Hearts Be Fertile Ground") that was intended to honor both Gary and Vickie.

Soon afterward, I was commissioned to write a hymn for the commemoration of the tenth anniversary of Rev. Sarah Jackson Shelton's pastorate at Baptist Church of the Covenant in Birmingham, Alabama. Because of Rev. Shelton's gift for effectively utilizing stories to illustrate her sermons, I was again drawn to the parables of Jesus as a source of inspiration. For this occasion, I was able to learn that Rev. Shelton's favorite parable was the story of the prodigal son and wrote "Who Was the Prodigal?" for that occasion.

From those two texts I embarked on a scriptural search for other parables of Jesus that might stimulate ideas for additional hymn texts that could be useful in providing for congregations appropriate sung responses to the reading of and/or preaching on the respective parables. This small collection is the result of that search and the new hymn texts that emerged from it.

New tunes were written for two of the parable-based texts. Tune suggestions are offered for the others. For one text ("How Much Is Enough?"), no tune suggestion is provided, since the text is in an unusual meter for which I was unable to locate what I considered to be a suitable tune. Therefore, it is available to stimulate creative work from a current tune writer.

I am grateful to my long-time colleague and friend, Dr. Paul Richardson, for reviewing these texts and offering insightful suggestions for revision.

Matthew 13:1-8, 18-23

That same day Jesus went out of the house and sat by the lake. Great crowds gathered around him, so he got into a boat and sat in it, while all the people stood on the shore. Then he told them many things in parables, saying:

"A sower went out to sow his seed. As he was scattering the seed, some fell along the path, and the birds came and ate them. Some fell on rocky places, where there was not much soil. They sprang up quickly, because the soil was shallow. But when the sun came up, the plants were scorched, and they withered because they had no root. Other seed fell among thorns, which grew up and choked the plants. Still other seed fell on good soil, where they produced a crop—a hundred, sixty, or thirty times what was sown."

—

"Listen, then, to what the parable of the sower means: When anyone hears the message about the kingdom and does not understand it, the evil one comes and snatches away what was sown in the heart. This is the seed sown along the path. The one who received the seed that fell on rocky places is the person who hears the word and at once receives it with joy. But since it is not rooted, when trouble or persecution comes because of the word, he quickly falls away. The one who receives the seed that fell among the thorns is the person who hears the word, but the cares of this life and the deceitfulness of wealth choke the word, making it unfruitful. But the one who received the seed that fell on good soil is the person who hears the word and understands it, yielding fruit that is a hundred, sixty or thirty times what was sown."

Lord, May Our Hearts Be Fertile Ground

Matthew 13:1-23; Mark 4:1-20; Luke 8:4-15

Lord, may our hearts be fertile ground
as we receive Your fruitful word,
and let not sin in us abound,
lest we neglect the truth we've heard.

Deliver us from faint belief
and superficiality,
and let Your word be rooted deep
so we withstand adversity.

May riches, cares, or ill desire
not choke the faith within our hearts,
but by Your Spirit so inspire
that we mature what grace imparts.

Embolden us to speak Your word
and so proclaim its truth, that we,
as faithful servants of our Lord,
both sowers and receivers be.

TUNE: FURR (LM)
ALTERNATE TUNE: CANONBURY

Milburn Price

Luke 10:25-37

On one occasion an expert in the law stood up and, in order to tempt Jesus, asked, "Teacher, what must I do to inherit eternal life?"

"What is written in the law?" Jesus replied. "How do you read it?"

He answered: "Love the Lord your God with all your heart and with all your soul and with all your strength and with all your mind; and love your neighbor as yourself."

Jesus replied, "You have answered correctly. Do this and you will live."

But the man wanted to justify himself, so he asked Jesus, "And who is my neighbor?" Jesus answered by saying: "A man was going down from Jerusalem to Jericho, when he fell into the hands of thieves, who stripped his clothes from him, beat him, and went away, leaving him half dead. A priest came along the same road, and when he saw the man, he passed by on the other side. Likewise, a Levite, when he came to the place and saw him, passed by on the other side. But a certain Samaritan, as he traveled, came where the man was; and when he saw him, he had compassion for him. He went to the man and bandaged his wounds, pouring on oil and wine. He set the man on his donkey, took him to an inn, and took care of him. The next day, when he departed, he took out two coins, gave them to the innkeeper, and said, 'Take care of him, and when I return, I will repay you for any additional expense.' Which of these three do you think was a neighbor to the man who fell into the hands of thieves?" The expert in the law replied, "The one who showed mercy to him." Jesus said to him, "Go and do likewise."

Who Is My Neighbor?

Luke 10:25-37, with allusion to Matthew 25:40, 45

Who is my neighbor? How near or how far
am I expected to go to show care?
Whatever distance, wherever needs are,
I know, O God, You are already there.

Who is my neighbor? How much and how long
does Your commandment require that I give?
Your teaching, clearly persuasive and strong,
calls me to share so that others may live.

Who is my neighbor? How many or few
should I include in my outreach of love?
"Unto the least of these"—Your words ring true,
 shaping Your kingdom both here and above.

Help us be sensitive to those in need:
homeless and hungry, bereft, or in pain;
may we adopt "the Samaritan's creed"—
helping and giving . . . and giving again.

SUGGESTED TUNE:
SLANE (10.10.10.10)

Milburn Price

Matthew 25:31-46

"When the Son of Man comes in his glory, and all the angels with him, he will sit upon his heavenly throne. All the nations will be gathered before him, and he will separate the people as a shepherd divides his sheep from the goats. He will place the sheep on his right hand and the goats at his left.

"Then the king will say to those on his right hand, 'Come you who are blessed by my Father, inherit the kingdom prepared for you from the foundation of the world. For I was hungry, and you gave me meat; I was thirsty and you gave me something to drink; I was a stranger and you took me in, naked and you clothed me; I was sick and you visited me; I was in prison and you came to see me.'

"Then the righteous will answer him, 'Lord, when did we see you hungry and feed you, or thirsty and give you something to drink? When did we see you a stranger and take you in, or naked and clothe you? When did we see you sick or in prison and come to visit you?'

"And the king will answer, 'Truly I say to you, whenever you did it for one of the least of these my children, you did it for me.'

"Then he will say to those at his left, 'Depart from me, you who are accursed, into everlasting fire prepared for the devil and his angels. For I was hungry and you gave me nothing to eat; I was thirsty and you gave me nothing to drink; I was a stranger and you did not take me in, naked and you did not clothe me; I was sick and in prison and you did not visit me.'

"Then they will say, 'Lord, when did we see you hungry, or thirsty, or a stranger, or naked, or sick, or in prison and did not minister to you?'

"He will answer, 'Truly I say to you, whatever you did not do for one of the least of these, you did not do for me.'

"These will go away to everlasting punishment, but the righteous into eternal life."

O Lord, Your Word Has Come to Us

Matthew 25:31-46, with allusion to John 21:17

O Lord, Your word has come to us
   to stir us from our ease,
for we are called to minister
   "unto the least of these."

To whom, O Lord, are we to go
   in order to fulfill
the calling of our Christian task
   that carries out Your will?

To those who hunger, those who thirst,
   and all who are in need
Your word bids us to go in love,
   for Your flock we must feed.

"Unto the least of these": O Lord,
   in these, Your words, we find
a challenge that compels us forth
   in service to mankind.

SUGGESTED TUNE:
ST. ANNE (CM)

Milburn Price

Luke 18:1-8

Jesus told his disciples a parable to teach them that they should always pray and not give up, saying: "In a certain town there was a judge who neither feared God nor was concerned about people. There was a widow in that town who came to him, asking, 'Give me justice from my adversary.'

"For a while the judge refused, but after a time he said to himself, 'Though I do not fear God or care about people, because this widow persists with her request, I will give her justice so that she will not weary me with her coming.'"

And the Lord said, "Listen to what the unjust judge says. And will not God give justice to his own chosen ones who cry unto him day and night? I tell you that he will see that they get justice quickly. However, when the Son of Man comes, will he find faith on the earth?"

Praying Christ, We Hear Your Word

Luke 18:1-8, with allusion to Matthew 7:7-8 and Luke 11:9-10

Praying Christ, we hear Your word
call us to persistent prayer,
that Your will be undeterred
and Your justice we may share.
Often, with uplifted eyes,
may our prayers to You arise.

With the faith of true belief,
when life brings us grief or care
we will come to seek relief,
knowing that You hear our prayer.
Often, with uplifted eyes,
may our prayers to You arise.

Asking, we beseech, implore;
seeking for our cares to cease,
knocking at Your open door,
we await Your promised peace.
Often, with uplifted eyes,
may our prayers to You arise.

SUGGESTED TUNE:
DIX (7.7.7.7.7.7)

Milburn Price

Mark 4:30-34a

Jesus said, "What shall we say the kingdom of God is like, or with what parable shall we explain it? It is like a mustard seed, which is the smallest seed you plant in the ground. Yet, when planted, it grows and becomes the largest of all garden plants, with such big branches that the birds of the air can rest under its shadow." With many such parables Jesus spoke the word to them, to the extent they were able to understand. He did not say anything to them without using a parable.

From Tiny Seed of Mustard

Matthew 13:31-32, Mark 4:30-32, Luke 13:18-19

From tiny seed of mustard
   a verdant plant can grow;
so from Your planted word, Lord,
   can living faith o'er-flow.
The spreading of Your kingdom
   in each new heart and place
gives witness to the power
   of Your love and Your grace.

Fire our imaginations
   to see how we can be
the ones by whom Your word, Lord,
   is sowed abundantly.
In words of care and witness
   and deeds that help and heal,
may we, through all our actions,
   Your kingdom work reveal.

SUGGESTED TUNE:
MERLE'S TUNE (7.6.7.6.D)

Milburn Price

Luke 15:1-7

Tax collectors and sinners gathered around Jesus to hear him. But the Pharisees and scribes murmured, saying, "This man sits with sinners and eats with them."

Jesus told them this parable, saying: "If one of you has a hundred sheep and loses one of them, does he not leave the ninety-nine and go seek the sheep that is lost until he finds it? And when he finds it, he joyfully places it on his shoulders. When he gets home, he calls his friends and neighbors together and says to them, 'Rejoice with me, for I have found my lost sheep.'

"I tell you that, similarly, there will be more joy in heaven over one sinner who repents than over ninety-nine righteous persons who do not need to repent."

Jesus, Shepherd of the Flock

Matthew 18:12-14; Luke 15:3-7

Jesus, shepherd of the flock,
keep us safe within Your care.
Guard us, in our daily lives,
from temptation, trial, or snare.

Should we wander from Your fold,
bring us safely home again.
With repentance for our sin,
in Your will may we remain.

As forgiven sinners all,
we will act upon Your word—
seeking others who are lost
that they, too, may be restored.

SUGGESTED TUNE:
INNOCENTS OR SEYMOUR (7.7.7.7.)

Milburn Price

Matthew 7:24-27, NIV

"Therefore, everyone who hears these words of mine and puts them into practice is like a wise man who built his house on the rock. The rain came down, the streams rose, and the winds blew and beat against that house; yet it did not fall, because it had its foundation on the rock.

"But everyone who hears these words of mine and does not put them into practice is like a foolish man who built his house on sand. The rain came down, the streams rose, and the winds blew and beat against that house, and it fell with a great crash."

You Should Build on Firm Foundations

Matthew 7:24-27; Luke 6:47-49

"You should build on firm foundations,"
   Jesus' teaching urges all,
so that, when beset by challenge,
   we can stand, avoiding fall.

Those whose lives have weaker footing
   find themselves unfit to cope
with life's trials and temptations,
   without strength and without hope.

Lord, prepare us for the tempest,
   so that when we suffer stress
we are strengthened by the promise
   of Your love and faithfulness.

SUGGESTED TUNE:
RESTORATION (8.7.8.7)

Milburn Price

Matthew 25:14-29

"The kingdom of heaven will be like a man going on a journey who called his servants and entrusted his goods to them. To one he gave five talents of money, to another two talents, and to another one talent, to each man according to his ability. Then he went on his journey.

"The man who had received five talents put his money to work and gained five more. Likewise, the man who had received two talents gained two more. But the man who had received one talent went and dug in the ground and hid his master's money.

"After a long time the master of those servants returned and settled accounts with them. The man who had received five talents came, bringing the additional five talents, and said, 'Master, you entrusted me with five talents. See, I have gained five talents more.'

"His master said to him, 'Well done, good and faithful servant. You have been faithful over a few things; I will put you in charge of many things. Come and share your master's joy.'

"The man who had received two talents came and said, 'Master, you entrusted me with two talents. See, I have gained two talents more.'

"His master said to him, 'Well done, good and faithful servant. You have been faithful over a few things; I will put you in charge of many things. Come and share your master's joy.'

"Then the man who had received the one talent came and said, 'Master, I knew that you are a hard man, reaping where you have not sown and gathering where you have not scattered seed. So I was afraid and went and hid your talent in the ground. Here is what belongs to you.'

"His master said to him, 'You wicked, lazy servant, you knew that I reap where I have not sown and gathered where I have not scattered seed. Therefore, you should have put my money on deposit, so that when I returned I would receive it back with interest. Take the talent from him and give it to the man who has the ten talents. For to everyone who has will be given more, and he will have an abundance; and for those who do not have, even what they have will be taken away.'"

Take What I Give and Use It Well
Matthew 25:14-30

"Take what I give and use it well,"
the words of Jesus seem to say.
But how do we apply these words
to our own lives and work today?

Our work, possessions, talents, time
are all entrusted to our care
to use productively for God
and with our neighbors, too, to share.

No gift too small, no talent lost
to one who would Christ's servant be,
but by God's grace each gift is blessed
for those who serve God faithfully.

O God, may we aspire to be
the faithful stewards You desire.
Come, journey with us as we go…
our faith sustain, our work inspire.

SUGGESTED TUNE: VOM HIMMEL HOCH (L.M.)
ALTERNATE TUNE: LATHAM

Milburn Price

Luke 12:13-21

Someone in the crowd said to Jesus, "Master, tell my brother that he should divide the inheritance with me."

Jesus responded, "Man, who made me a judge or an arbiter between you?" Then he said to them, "Beware of covetousness; a man's life does not consist of the abundance of his possessions."

Then he spoke this parable: "The land of a certain rich man produced a good crop, and he thought to himself, 'What shall I do, for I have insufficient space to store my crops?'

"Then he said, 'This is what I'll do. I will tear down my barns and build bigger ones, and there I will store all my crops and goods. And I will say to myself, 'You have an abundance of good things stored up for many years. Enjoy your ease; eat, drink, and be merry.'

"Then God said to him, 'You fool, this night your life will be taken from you. Then who will get the things that you have provided for yourself?'

"So it will be for anyone who stores up things for himself but is not rich toward God."

How Much Is Enough?

Luke 12:13-21

How much is enough to sustain and provide
adequate comfort, provisions, and place
when there are others whose needs are denied
due to their circumstance, status, or race?

How much is too much to acquire and to hoard
for current use and for years far ahead
when there are others who cannot afford
life's basic needs, such as shelter and bread?

O God, may our outlook on money and things
be guided by a view deep faith supplies;
give us perspective discipleship brings
so that we see ourselves as through Your eyes.

(11.10.10.10)

Milburn Price

Luke 15:11-32

Jesus said, "There was a man who had two sons. The younger son said to his father, 'Father, give to me my share of your possessions.' So the father divided his property between them.

"Not many days after that, the younger son gathered all he had and made a journey to a distant country, where he wasted his wealth on profligate living. When he had spent everything, a severe famine came in that land, and he became needy. So he went and hired himself to a citizen of that country, who sent him into his fields to feed pigs. He would have filled his stomach with the husks that the pigs were eating, for no one gave him anything.

"When he came to his senses, he said, 'How many of my father's hired servants have more than enough food, and I am dying from hunger! I will go to my father and say to him: Father, I have sinned against heaven and against you, and am no longer worthy to be called your son. Let me be as one of your hired servants.' So he arose and went to his father.

"While he was still some distance away, his father saw him and had compassion for him; he ran to him, hugged him, and kissed him. The son said to his father, 'Father, I have sinned against heaven and against you, and am no longer worthy to be called your son.'

"But the father said to his servants, 'Bring the best robe and put it on him; put a ring on his finger and shoes on his feet. Bring the fattened calf and kill it, and let us eat and celebrate. For this, my son, was dead and is alive again; he was lost and is found.' So they began to celebrate.

"The elder son had been in the field, and when he neared the house, he heard music and dancing. So he called one of the servants and asked him the meaning of the celebration. The servant responded, 'Your brother has returned, and your father has killed the fattened calf because he has come back safely.'

"The elder brother became angry and would not go in, so his father came to him and pleaded with him. But he answered his father, saying, 'All these years

I have served you and never disobeyed your orders. Yet, you never gave me even a young goat so that I could celebrate with my friends. But when this son of yours returns, who has wasted your wealth with prostitutes, you kill the fattened calf for him.'

"The father said to him, 'My son, you are always with me, and all that I have is yours. It is fitting that we should celebrate and be glad, because your brother was dead and is alive again; he was lost and now is found.'"

Who Was the Prodigal?

Luke 15:11-32

Who was the prodigal? Was it the younger son—
   he who claimed his estate so he could roam?
After extravagant spending and wastefulness,
   his plight then prompted him to return home.

Who was the prodigal? Was it the elder son
   in his response to his brother's return?
Springing from jealousy for a perceived affront,
   he felt resentment within his heart burn.

See how the father, with love and with tenderness,
   deals with each child with forgiveness and grace,
lavishing mercy and offering blessing with
   great celebration, each wrong to erase.

O loving God, like a welcoming parent, now
   gladly receive us as we come to You.
Turn us from waywardness, forgive our selfishness,
   pardon our sin, and a deep faith renew.

TUNE: COVENANT (12.10.12.10)

Milburn Price

Lord, May Our Hearts Be Fertile Ground

WORDS: Milburn Price (based on Luke 8:4-15)
MUSIC: Milburn Price
© 2008 Celebrating Grace, Inc.

FURR
8.8.8.8

Who Was the Prodigal?

1. Who was the prod-i-gal? Was it the young-er son — he who claimed his es-tate so he could roam? Af-ter ex-trav-a-gant spend-ing and waste-ful-ness, his plight then prompt-ed him to re-turn home.
2. Who was the prod-i-gal? Was it the el-der son in his re-sponse to his broth-er's re-turn? Spring-ing from jeal-ou-sy from a per-ceived af-front, he felt re-sent-ment with-in his heart burn.
3. See how the fa-ther, with love and with ten-der-ness, deals with each child with for-give-ness and grace, lav-ish-ing mer-cy and of-fer-ing bless-ing with great cel-e-bra-tion, each wrong to e-rase.
4. O lov-ing God, like a wel-com-ing par-ent, now glad-ly re-ceive us as we come to You. Turn us from way-ward-ness, for-give our self-ish-ness, par-don our sin, and a deep faith re-new.

WORDS: Milburn Price
MUSIC: Milburn Price
© 2012 Celebrating Grace, Inc.

COVENANT
12.10.12.10

www.ingramcontent.com/pod-product-compliance
Lightning Source LLC
Chambersburg PA
CBHW020034120526
44588CB00030B/441